Chant of a

MILLION
WOMEN

By the Same Author

Breaking News (Vijitha Yapa, 2011) (*Short Stories*)

Chant of a
MILLION
WOMEN

SHIRANI RAJAPAKSE

Published by Shirani Rajapakse

Cover image by Shirani Rajapakse
Cover designed by FayeFayeDesigns
https://www.fiverr.com/fayefayedesigns

First Published in 2017

Paperback: ISBN: 978-955-38285-0-7
eBook: ISBN: 978-955-38285-1-4

1. Poetry. 2. Poems—21st century. 3. Women. 4. Woman—power. 5. Woman—abuse. 6. Asian Writer. 7. Shirani Rajapakse.

For information about permission to reproduce selections from this book, or to translate, write to
shiraniraj@hotmail.com
shiranirajapakse@gmail.com
https://shiranirajapakse.wordpress.com

To
my grandmother,
my mother,
and
my aunts.

Acknowledgements

Acknowledgements are due to the following print and online journals, and anthologies where these poems first appeared:

Asian Cha, Hong Kong (*Questions Left Unanswered* – Winner, 'Betrayal' Poetry Contest 2013); Asian Signature, India (*Unwanted Visitors*); Berfrois, UK (*At the Café*); Dagda, UK (*Alone One Evening*); Dove Tales, USA (*Lost in Thought*); Earthen Lamp Journal, India (*Dream of the Housemaid, Loneliness*); Lakeview, India (*Earth Song*); Mascara Literary Review, Australia (*Games People Play*); New Verse News, USA/Indonesia (*Occupy Wall Street)*; Poetica Magazine, USA (*The Shower* - Finalist, Anna Davidson Rosenberg Award 2013); Poet's Basement, USA (*Misunderstanding*); Skylight 47, Ireland (*Unwanted*); Verses in Motion, USA (*I Live in Dreams*- radio show); Voices Israel Poetry, Israel (*The Violinist*); Wordshark blog, USA (*Inside the Old Room*).

With thanks to

Dr. Lakshmi de Silva,
lecturer and mentor,
for helping select the poems for this
collection and the many years of advice.

Contents

At the Side of the Old Mandir

They come to this place every day
to touch you.
Lonely men with desires unfulfilled.
Can't afford the real thing, costs too much
these days, a glance, a caress.
They can barely afford food for the day.

You're the best they can have;
voluptuousness in stone.
They ogle and marvel, then
gradually draw nearer.
A furtive glance in every direction to check
if anyone's watching and a hand
lifts up to cup a breast.
Human and rock merge for a blissful moment.
An eternity passes as time
drags itself to a screeching halt.
Sighs of contentment escape.

Satiated temporarily,
they return to a place at a distance,
to admire and hope.

Later, moving inside they speak to God, plead
with him, cajole, sometimes demand.
Karma always questioned in times like this.
A truth hard to accept.
The reasons why never defined, lying hidden
in the cosmic ether beyond their
comprehension.

Your breasts are a shade darker than
the rest of your body,
colored from constant caresses of
lonesome men seeking stolen pleasures.
A slow smile playing on your lips, one arm
resting on a hip pushed out to the side,
the other raised from the elbow,
fingers encircling lotus, you stand waiting
for what might be, as they shuffle past,
circumambulating
like the devout, softly singing praise
of the one within.
Quietly taking in their fill they return to
homes devoid of love and desire.

Who are you,
proud woman standing nonchalantly
gazing into the distance as they walk past?
What was your fate?
Willed by the hand that chiseled
you from a large rock hewn out from
another place one sunny day eons ago.
Who was the man that yearned for you so,
he cast you in stone in remembrance
to watch over the years
and give hope to
a multitude of desperate souls?

I Live in Dreams

I live in dreams.
I walk on asphalt. Hard and dry.
Yet I soar. My mind unfettered by
the claiming of reality.

I live in two worlds, one
real and the other almost real.
They mingle into each other
sometimes making it hard
to define each one.

My dreams ease the burden
of life, tough as the asphalt that
hurt the soles of my feet as
they trudge along, day in, day out.
Is there no release from
this reality, this pain?

Except in dreams, when I live
I am me. The real person I
was meant to be.
But cannot be.
Reality hems me in defining
life as it should be.
Not as it ought to be.

Lost in Thought

She stared at the people passing on
the street before her. A myriad
colors and shapes
wafted by, some hurrying some moving
slowly, but all going somewhere.

She moved with them,

although her feet did not leave the space
she was in. She sat there staring,
but her mind was rushing faster
than the people on the street.
Where was she going?
She wasn't sure, but knew she
wanted to get away from here. To be there;

somewhere, wherever. She didn't hear

the door behind her creak open, then softly
close. It always made those sounds.
She didn't hear him speak,
call out to her as he shut the door. She
was far away, in a place he could not enter.

Not now. Not ever.

To Dance with the Wind

Head uncovered, wisps of breeze scurry
through hair free to dance as it pleases.
Burrowing deep, lifting off scalp, picking up
strands, the breeze controls the movements
to an unheard beat no one can discern.

You have
no idea what choices you've got.

She remembered that lighthearted feeling
many years ago,
a child playing in the old home
unruffled by the strain of adulthood, shaded
by tall trees that bent branches to tap
beats in the air performing to a
silent conductor of the zephyr orchestra.

Those moments rare as precious stones
hidden beneath swirling waters
in rivers that rushed away.

It lasted only for so long.

Now, a black shroud covers it all,
hiding her thick long tresses from sight.
Winds beat against cloth walls trying
to free hairs cowering in shame,
calling out to come perform to the melody of
a new sonata composed that day.
Slits for her eyes that once mesmerized,
peepholes to the world that you look at
without fear of someone, anyone,
turning your life into
a pile of flesh and bone at

the stroke of a whim.
Longing to run free through unpaved roads
the grass on either side tickling toes,
pebbles poking soles of feet through rubber
slippers to leave imprints that faded in time,
run like she did as a child,
the wind in her hair, lifting them
higher and higher like
when she flew through the air on the swing
her grandfather hung on the tree,
but her feet are held back by invisible chains.

You don't understand, living over there
so far away in another world; think it's a fad,
being with the crowd, this covering up in
shrouds, like the dead thrown
inside the earth to rot in silence; wanting
to look a certain way, be considered religious,
or whatever that means to you.
Don't stop to think how she yearns
for what you have, the power of choice,
freedom to be who you want to be.
But you want to be

no one, an invisible thing

hidden behind a black wall while
all she wants is to soar with the winds,
graze the clouds, turn her face to the sun,
let her curls dance, dance, dance
like a myriad hands moving out to catch
pieces of the sun, her feet
stamping a beat as she flies away from here to
someplace else where she can be herself.

The person she was meant to be.

On the Way Home

They made a movie on a bus
riding around town.
No one heard the songs, or saw
the dances. The action stars were new.

Later, someone threw in a name —Nirbhaya.

On and on they moved around Delhi's leafy
avenues, curtains drawn while the engine
kept time to the sounds inside.
No cuts, no breaks, the actors
played their part.
The heroine protested—like all heroines do.
A new face she was dressed for the part,
an item girl, they sang as she danced.
Munirka to Dwarka it purred on its way.

The wheels turned round and round
as the winter chill crept through
the leaves on the trees and a single leaf
fluttered to the ground, torn apart.
It fell across the road and no one took note.

Just another leaf among so many in the city.

Action spent, the bus came to a stop, but
before they could shoot again the city rose in
wrath to demand a ban on the script's repeat.
Candles lit, they waited it out, but
the wheels grind slowly round and round.
And while the old men argued
in vain inside colonial walls another

leaf fell silently to the ground.

Unwanted

You placed me
on a shelf and left me there
to dry. I was forgotten.
Like the old newspaper you
spread on your
writing table to protect
the wood. It turned yellow in time
and you threw it away
one day, not so long ago.
I too have faded.
Would you
throw me out too?

Occupy Wall Street

Sweat
streams down her cheeks
and loses itself
in her blouse.
There's time yet
for her to leave. The clock ticks.
Her eyes hurt.
Her hands
feel numb. Is this life?
She has no choice.
It's her day.
Darkness all
around, sweating it out
for a morsel
of food for her family
waiting patiently for
her return.
Her fingers ache.
The machine throbs in
her head.
She lifts her hand
to wipe off
the sweat.
*Wall Street's
occupied,* drones the
newsreader.
She looks up, but
doesn't understand.
Then back
to the machine.

Colonized

Lipstick stained your shirt a deep
luscious pink. Mine.
I opened lips
and drank you in. The leftovers
fell on your shirt and stained it pink.

I suppose that's what happened.
I don't remember
how it got there, but there it was
looking like a ripe dragon-fruit stuck
to the side of your shirt—white,
stark, blazing a mark in bold pink.

Layers and layers
of succulence, thick sensuous lips
opening up, panting, thirsting,
drinking you in.
You were marked.
Stamped with delicious dragon-fruit
pink.
Scandalous.

Mine.

Branded like a buffalo in the field.
So domesticated—almost.
Everyone turned
to see, but you didn't care or seem to mind.
Captured, acquired, taken. You were

sold and it was I that bought.

She Thought She Knew it All

Poetry for the masses, that's what
she wrote. It was like the public bus, serving
everyone and no one.

People got on people got off.
The woman carrying vegetables to
the local fair;
the cripple looking for handouts;
the beggar sticking out his hand for
a few coins to drown his sorrows;
schoolboys riding to school;
people on their way to work.

They couldn't afford the luxury of private cars,
they traveled stuck tight among the public.

She wrote for the masses, that's
what they said.
Kept her volume beside their bed,
inside their bags, read her whenever they
could, just to commune with the rest
and feel solace that someone
empathized in a world
full of no meaning.

But that's all she was.
No one else gave a damn.

They rode in cars with tinted glass.

They read a different verse.
She was not counted.
But she didn't know.
Ignorance is such bliss.

In the House at the End of the Road

She plucked
her breasts because
she said they didn't fit.
She was
meant to be male, but

they had grown on their own,
large and voluminous
sticking out for all to see like buoys in the sea.
Obstinate, rude and beckoning
to all. *Come see me*
defy the rules.

I stand up to gravity.

They cramped her style.
She couldn't move her arms
or bend down to touch
the ground.

So she ripped them out,
one by one.
Unlike the Amazons, they only removed one.
It was an occupational hazard.
That's what they said.

They couldn't aim their bows
to defend their realm.
But she had nothing to defend.
Except her annoyance at
being female.

The Violinist

Lifting, moving,
bowing. I saw her
move many years ago.
It seemed like yesterday, or so
my memory said.

Blue stripes
on loose white covered skin
and bone too young to look
like that. Old and gnarled
like trees in a
garden somewhere nice.

She steadied her
arm and lifted again.

The star gleamed on
translucent skin.
I remembered.
Dark, black with numbers
to count. Her days
were numbered. One.
Two. Three.

She knew. I saw.

The music rose
from her bow. She
played. They played
with her. I tried to follow.
Another performance.
Another day to live.
Cold, shivering, yet the
bow moved up then

down as the music
moved the audience to tears.
Medals gleamed,
while hearts bled, yet
she lived another day.
While all around fell
to his command.

Misunderstanding

He's lying in a hospital bed.
She doesn't know.

Three days she hasn't heard from him.
The phone's been silent. Her mind drifts

to unwanted places.
She sees him with another, doing things

they used to do.
Her mind plays games,

yet she doesn't want to pick up
the phone, unsure of what he'd say.

Unsure of who would pick up,
a stranger's voice she doesn't want to hear

while on the other side of town
he waits, wondering what

has taken her so long.
Has she lost interest so soon?

He looks at the phone and wonders
if she's with someone else.

The pain moves to his heart, but something
holds him back. Life drifts past

like trains in the dark.

Standing My Ground

Sometimes
it's that little extra ingredient you
add at the last minute that
matters to the taste.
The recipe has it all, but
a little something thrown in on a whim
alters the flavor.

That's me,
being an individual,

not one in the crowd that's
made to dance to the same
communal tunes played
over and over and over
till everyone drops dead of exhaustion.
Creating variations I add my own strings,
a twang here and there,
an interlude where I desire.
My seal of ingenuity.
My stamp blazing a trail across the land.

But no one notices in the millions
surging forward that
I stand my ground, refusing to
move an inch, waiting as I am, here,
in the middle of a busy highway,
traffic swirling around like white water,
my face lifted to the sun shining down
through diaphanous clouds flittering by,
bathing me in gold and orange while
all others rush
to an unseen future
playing to the same old beat.

At the Café

I didn't see it coming.
My cup was full and overflowing.

You picked at your food, staring over
my head at the big screen in
the corner playing old movies to

an empty café. Mesmerized

you watched scenes unfold somewhere
in the middle of a conversation
with no care for the person in
front of you.

"It's not you, it's me," you said later, when
it was all over. It was easier over the phone.
No emotions; tears to wipe,
no scenes from a movie best left out.
Just words, impersonal, droned down the wire.
Another dimension.

The coffee in my cup tasted bad, end of
a relationship before it went sour
like old milk way past its time.

Rust coffee, you joked one day about
the fungus infecting the plantations far away.
"You will not have your coffee next year,"

but your smile didn't reach your eyes.
It hovered at the corners of your lips and
disappeared, embarrassed at
being seen in public.

And that was it.
You ran out faster than the coffee.
Sitting by my side
on the drive back home we spoke in silence.

The wind blew our words to
the next town
where you will go to play the part
all over again.

The Way Back

There's that hollow you hide
inside when things get out of hand, too
loud those noises around, voices shrill like
pieces of broken glass you
stepped on,
the cuts leaving a trail of red drops
on the cement floor.
Rose petals strewn all over like when
they were blown off the stems
in the garden by
the wild monsoon last year.
They dried out with the wind, growing darker
against the gray of the fractured floor.
Your feet, wiped with an old rag,
doused in disinfectant.

They wouldn't understand although you
try to explain those moments
of bliss before gray
clouds rush in to block
the sun coming through.
Her golden fingers scratch the surface then
move away
disappointed at being rejected.

If only you could remember
the way back to that time long ago.

The cracks in your mind widening, getting
longer like evening shadows stretching
themselves into the night.
The lengthy pauses
when you search for words that have
trickled out through little spaces like

water falling
from fissures in dried old leaves
that have lost their color
and form yet linger for nature's next move.

You huddle in that space surrounded by
swirling darkness staring out at nothing while
morsels of hope sit
on the edge of your tongue
waiting for directions from the wind
that has tired of calling out your name.

Dream of the Housemaid

Returning home on a stretcher,
a plane ride to the desert many months ago
gone so wrong.
You got much more than you bargained for,
with a salary paid in nails.

Hard as hell.

Forced inside, damming your veins,
piercing bones, rotting, festering.
Tears all dried up, you came back in pain.
Dreams shattered,
leaving them scattered in the sands for
scavengers to feast.

The oil merchant's wife made sure of it.

There was something she didn't like, or maybe
he didn't like being rejected. Wasn't used to it.

They held you down on
a chair in the kitchen writhing and
howling in pain, nails
hammered in, one at a time.
Your hands, your feet, as you cried out in vain.

Stuffed some down your throat until
you were too full of it all.
The X-rays back home confirmed, but
oh the shame. No one believed. No one.

Your story was good, made the news
that night and the next day too.
Everyone had something to say.

But no one believed.
The press was amused; you made it all up,
someone sniggered. Couldn't handle
the pressure, the agency that sent you
grumbled and ignored your plea.

Said you did it for a
piece of fame; time in the spotlight.
But what a show. You got nothing, nothing.

Alone on a hospital bed swathed
in bandages, stuffed with medication, they
stare and talk in whispers as you
recollect the journey to the Middle East,
oasis of the poor.
You went to make money, like
everyone else in the village, build a house,
educate your three children waiting at home
with their grandmother.
Your husband a drunkard, he couldn't
keep a job, so you took over. They had to live.
But all you got were nails beaten in
like Jesus that day.

Yet where's your cross?
Where are your followers?

Money gone,
dignity in shreds you yearn to return
as unfulfilled dreams refuse to leave,
tugging at your heart, calling,
calling to come
finish what you started.

Mutilated

Lips inviting, delicious pink, sealed shut.

Words are dammed, can barely trickle out.
Sewn up tight, threads crisscross, an ugly
design like embroidery by
an unknown hand done hurriedly,
no attempt to please.
No one's permitted inside
tiny dark spaces except those with a key.

Lips are fastened together. Locked up
tight, she finds it hard
to sing sweet songs of longing.
Can only hum softly to herself about
things you cannot understand, like
monthly rituals, prayers at the altar you
sometimes visit to worship on open days, yet
on others decline, annoyed,
standing waiting in line for many days.
The road blocked,
there's a bottleneck to the exit.
Traffic builds up each month like panic times
at the petrol station when prices skyrocket
and everyone wants to fill up.
Or pass the time at
some border waiting to cross over, get their
papers stamped - an approval, hanging
around until the gates open
and they are authorized entry.

Lips are closed.

A diminutive space,
just a little to let the world know she's alive,
imprisoned, hurting.
A little breath of fresh air allowed to amble in,
sometimes, rather surreptitiously.

Lips secured shut. She can only murmur.
Teardrops trickle red mud, garnets winking
from the bowels of the earth, painting
horizons like the setting sun blazing
across the world, vermillion tears
in the rain, running all over.

Lips you yearn to kiss, mold
to your being. Soft, pliable rubies
hidden forever from view.

Chant of a Million Women

My body is a temple, not
a halfway house you enter for
temporary shelter from
the heat and dust swirling through trees.
It's not a guest house to book a room, spend
a night on your way to someplace else.
Not a transit lounge
to while away the hours until
your next flight to fantasy seeking
greener pastures.

My body is my temple.

Enter with reverence.

Keep your shoes at the door your
hat on the step. Bring flowers as offering.
Garlands of jasmine wound tight, pink
lotus piled up high on a tray, petals opened,
lips inviting, alluring.

Place oil lamps on the floor.
Let the light guide the way, chase away
shadows trying to hide in gloomy corners.

Burn sweet incense, let the perfume linger
on the air, climb on the tail of a
gust of breeze
and travel unhindered.

Murmur sutras to supplicate.
Sing songs of praise.
Call out my many names amassed
down the ages.

Place those trays of fresh fruit,
succulent, ripe and oozing, at the side.
My body is my own.

Not yours to take
when it pleases you, or
use as collateral in the face
of wars fought for your greed, or zest to own.
Not give to appease the enemy, reward
the brave who sported so valiantly in the
trenches, stinking of blood and gore.

It's not a product.
Not something to bargain, barter for goods
and services, share with friends,
handed around the table,
a bowl of soup, drink your fill,
use and abuse as you please.

Don't adorn me in expensive silks and gold,
and gift to the Gods, or
wrap me up in a shroud,
imprison me, maim my thoughts
that shout to get out.
No religious decree, no social pressure,
you have no right to own.

It's mine and mine alone and you have
no authority to take it away from me.

The Closet Rapist

The black smudge was when she
walked into a door, she mumbles avoiding
my eye. Cut herself while cooking,
explaining the line
snaking across her left arm below
the elbow, like a road cut hurriedly through
the undergrowth chopping
down surprised trees.
She's left-handed, couldn't clarify the
sudden need to
change hands to hold a knife.
She turns away,
bites her lip to hide the old cut there.
Must have chewed her lip again sometime,
but couldn't recall.
So long ago, she smiles wanly to walls that
scream answers in silence to the air.

Other scars hidden far away behind her eyes.
They peep out when no one's there,
don't dare step out.
Every day he has his way with her. Every

day.

Leaves nothing to show except the pain in
her eyes and the sudden withdrawal from life.

The garden outside the house
is neglected, vines spread out, swinging from
branches to hide the view, weeds smother
pleading grass; inside, the furniture
needs dusting.

The chair he threw at her
wobbles at the corner one leg unhinged.
Broken plates sit
at the back of the cupboard ashamed
of being seen in the garbage. Life moves on.
No one knows what takes place
in dark spaces when doors are shut
and curtains drawn.
People turn in for the night, lock their doors
from the inside. Sounds blaring from TVs
throughout the night muffle other sounds.

Who would have thought?
They look the perfect couple, young,
educated, good jobs,
everyone's envious of their life.

She wakes up from the
nightmares to face
another day, and
another as the world walks on smiling
past her, flowing like
a soundless stream.

Somewhere in the Middle East After One War Ended

Child in the classroom unable
to speak. Staring at the space in front
silent to the teachers urging.

Mouth refusing to shape
words that don't come out, they died,
crumbled to dust and got lost
in the sands swirling not so very long ago.

What thoughts hold her back afraid
to open lips that might howl out secrets
best left hidden amidst the ruins
piled up like garbage?

Numb to the people, deaf
to the voices moving around, she hears
strange noises in her mind
deafening the songs
trying to rise up from a corner where
she stored them for safe keeping,
to make her smile.

Gunshots in the street,

the heavy fire of machine guns in
the dark of the night, a river
roaring through
nonstop taking with it the trees
uprooted, buildings collapsed.

Flares lighting up the
sky as she hid under
the bed seeing neon signs flash across
the sky through a hole in the roof
that brought in the sun during the day,
hot and burning, like the sting of the bullet
in her mother's chest.

The guns are silenced for the moment,
only the distant low hum of
sporadic fire in some other town
not so far away.

People walk the streets unafraid, go about
their work like
nothing ever happened.
The past erased.

Yet the guns inside
her head continue to fire volley after volley
as she struggles to live each day.

Loneliness

Because I crossed over
no man's land one day, a few steps
of nothingness between two countries
that drew borders to fence us in.
A sliver of territory
just enough for a road to run through,
a few kiosks that might make it
livable, but not
sufficient for homes
to make you feel loved, or
to put down roots.

No one feels
at home in no man's land.

No one stops there. Not for long.
Only lonely birds swooping down infrequently
to rest awhile, taking wing as they sense
all is not quite right. Or
the occasional curious cow that wonders
if the grass is really greener
yet doesn't venture further.
A feeling of unease she can't quite understand;
fear of death by slaughter, slow and painful,
cold breeze carrying messages of anguish
and terror waiting on
the other side.

Because sometimes words
are not required to make one understand or
experience joy and grief
at the same time.

Because of this you left, unable
to comprehend, refused to accompany me.
Stood for an hour at the threshold until
the gates closed behind me.
You gazed as I went over
to the other country.
Past the entrance,
the men in uniform, the plumed hats,
the paperwork, the stamp of finality,
to get lost in the rest of what makes it theirs.

Not yours anymore.

Because it happened so long ago you
don't remember the words spoken
as you watched people
stride away. Like me.

But I remembered your face that day
and the words you
wanted to speak,
but couldn't,
so you let your eyes converse instead.
Because it sounded so good,
like a violin crying in an abandoned house,
like a dog howling in the lonely ruins,
like a peacock singing in a desert dream,
and I remembered.

The Shower

She waits for the water
to fall, to flow over and wash her clean
like the day she was born.
Together they journeyed across the land
travelling the distance long and hard.

Some died, crammed like cattle
inside carriages,
trampled on by others trying
to make room, or be comfortable.

But she lived, while they died.

She waits
for the water in that cold hard place.
Shivers run down her back
yet she smiles to herself in anticipation
of better things while all the rest
wait with her, wondering why the water
doesn't come. The showers have gone dry.
She looks down at the little
child standing
patiently by her side and sees
her smile mirrored with hope.
The future seems fine. They made it after all.
It couldn't be that bad.

Suddenly, the smell of gas.
All around they scream and gag.
She claws the air,
falling, crashing, never to rise again,
the smile wiped off her lips
now drawn with pain.

No One Wants to Know

It was only much later,
when the world had gone to sleep and
awoken many times, that they found out.
By then it was far too late.
People had moved on. Old news was of no use,
they yawned as they picked up the papers
delivered that morning to read the news
crisp and new. Someone lost a cat,
someone broke into a home.
No laws were needed for any of that, no urgent
appeals, that could wait.

But she was only five years old.

They are all silent, those people in high places.
They've run out of words, catch phrases they
threw out to the women in jest.

Wrong clothes, out in the dark alone
with a strange man. Of course they deserved it,
those stupid women, they said laughing
behind closed doors.
And now they are scratching their balls and
trying to come up with reasons where
reasons never existed for any of this.
But it's too late.

Too late for her, the little girl.

Too late for her sisters in other places.
Too late for the mothers whose
daughters died a slow painful death.
Too late, too late. But no one cares.
Not theirs to care.

The Lonely Woman

They jeered as she walked up the steps.
Her people, they forgot her so soon.

I stare at the portrait hung in her
old room and wonder.

Dressed in volumes of silk, staring into
my eyes as if trying to tell me

something
about herself they all chose to hide.

They called her a traitor throughout her
life, but all she did was try

to be the person she was
meant to be.

The rooms at Versailles carry her
signature style.

She looks out of the canvas, perhaps
she remembered the parties,
the soirees in the gardens,
the dresses, the food and
the many, many splendid nights
in dark corners.

I gaze from the window and
imagine how
it must have looked,

wishing I could have
been there, sipping champagne
and talking with the crowds,
my skirt billowing on the lawns like a mast
on the tropical sea or
standing here watching from
the shadows of the windows.

She gave them
cake when there was no bread,
but they forgot all that and only
wanted her head.

Calling out loud they threw rotten food at
her standing there in the
centre of it all,
dressed in a cheap white dress
coarse to the touch, her long hair cut short,
her neck to the block.

And as the stone rose up, up, up
and the blade came crashing down
on her neck,
she heard the applause rise
loud from the crowd
and smiled to herself as her head bounced,
once, twice and came to rest at the side.

It wasn't so bad after all.

Walking the World

She built a ladder to
the moon, bamboo sticks tied up tight.
It stretched itself tall, a tree hiding
itself in folds of gossamer clouds that
sometimes paused to lounge on its rungs.

She assembled a castle in
the air with dreams inside her head;
ideas and words that rose up in shapes of
brick, roofing sheets, wooden frames for
windows and doors. Sprawling gardens filled
with exotic flowers, araliya, pichcha and
orchids flirting with the breeze floating,
delicious perfumes in the air.

She moved mountains with her
thoughts bringing them crashing to her feet as
she stepped up to Annapurna, one tiny
footstep at a time. And as

she watched the sun attempt to scale the
peaks, the snow melted on her cheek starting
a stream that turned into a waterfall that
scurried down a cliff that
became a river that
ran, ran, ran into the ocean deep.

She glided across deserts and plains,
flapped her wings, swooped down to perch atop
a shady tree surveying the world below,
a hawk seeking its prey watching intently,
patiently. She hitched a ride on a
rain cloud thick and gray and dropped to
earth to start anew once more.

The Stray

*"Why take her? She's a
bitch,"* he sounded puzzled.
She stared at him,
astounded.

*"Your mother's
the same kind,"* she replied,
and took the homeless
bitch home.

Major Minority

I've got a vote, but
I can't use it. Can't make much of a difference.
I'm the major minority.

My words shouted out from
rooftops, strong as monsoon winds that
makes fools of trees, they flutter and stumble,
evaporating in the breeze.
Protests are as insignificant as tiny particles
of gray dust picked up under bird claws
and carried to
the other town.
Doors bang shut locking me
inside rooms, dark dungeons of silence.

No one's interested in what I need.
I could bleed to death, cover the floors
warm red wall to wall for all they cared.
Yet they tell me I'm strong, that
I can rule the world if I desire.
They empathize, sympathize, then apologize
for years of neglect, but despite it all,
you want me in the house
making clothes for children that have
come and gone long ago.
Cooking meals for memories past, talking to
walls and doors that close in on me.
Wrapped up in ugly shrouds to keep me
safe from you,
my protector.

Entombed from the womb
by man-made rules,
religious decrees you twist, like you did the
bougainvillea vine outside the window, to
suit your wishes and not any
God that ever was.

You amuse yourself in a childish game,
playing God almighty to trap me.

I have a voice, but
I can't use it, although
I scream out loud. I'm the major minority.
I'm struck dumb. I blabber in silence,
a lonely being trapped in a
fortress with no exits.

I'm the major minority bowing to your wishes.
A puppet to please, all dolled up to
entertain you like
a roadside attraction or
a talking parrot that will say all the
right words; the ones you want
to hear and nothing more.

I'm part of a group that's unable to
break free, I'm that major,
major minority.

Glass Shoes

You came with a mold, a pair of
glass shoes I had to fit myself into,
like some lonely woman in
a fairytale you read as a child.
Sparkling in the light, gold details enticing,
you thought I'd fall for your gifts
unquestioning.

Your words attached to the shoes
like some strange design tumbled out
thunder across the sky.
Your rules, a
long winding list, like the potholed road
swirling up a mountain I travelled
a long time ago,
that made me sick of the journey
even before it began.

I refused to play.
Declined to walk in tall stilettos with
my toes pinching like
a million ants in attack mode,
my back weighed down at every step.

You tried to break me like
a horse in some foreign stable you
once visited.

I couldn't be a slave to your
master command, thinly veiled by
your so-called modernity, the
worldliness you portrayed by your
cosmopolitan lifestyle.
Yet your mind dwelled deep inside

a cave in an ancient time
long forgotten by me,
but remembered so well by you,
the information guarded and
ideas nurtured within.
A Neanderthal in a business suit.
You were no different from the rest that
passed by my view, although I never
saw through it
until, until, until.

And then it was too late.

The glass ceiling restricted me, threw
me back every time I boldly took
a hammer to it, told me silently I could go
no further, until I walked
out, slammed the door, watched the glass
shatter into little pieces that reflected
my face like a million and one
photographs scattered on the floor, and
I started to live the way I chose.

Your glass shoes confined
and imprisoned me in
an invisible cage I never knew existed and
I'm still trying hard to break free, find
the door in this seamless place, my
song stuck, plastered to the walls of my heart,
my words crumbling, eggshells
in the silence, my voice
no longer recognizable and my
mind withered leaves
no one needs anymore.

Sigiriya

Where do your thoughts dwell as you
stand there dear sisters, amidst misty clouds
swirling, your fingers entwined with
pink lotus from ponds
beyond, the color of
your lips, your desire?

Do you think of the days
stretching before you like a long intricate
carpet from a country once visited,
that's rolled out to please,
and of lazing under tall shady trees along
well trodden lanes, their branches
spread out like dancers
in eternal pose, laden with fragrant blossoms
and fruit in abundance to please every
palate, and of the countless nights
of wondrous pleasures?
Moonlight dancing on trees,
stars flirting with clouds.

Or do you contemplate on
the transience of life or what might have been
had things remained the same as they were,
as you recalled?
Or does your mind stray
to something else completely?

Do you,
dear sisters, ever wonder what it might be like
to leave your post for just a day to live like us,
a pose you've struck for centuries
modeling a life we can only imagine?

People come and go, climbing the rock
admiring your beauty as you gaze
into the distance.
Dressed in splendor,
your abundant hair wound in
a style that's your own,
adorned with gold and pearls,
clothed in simple silks.

Do you cringe as the men gape at you,
topless and exposed to all,
or do lotus lips part, as
you smile that slow smile and dismiss?

Unwanted Visitors

          Voices rose inside
                your head
cutting me off.   I was of no
consequence
in the scheme
of things. They ruled.
                    I was left out.
Speaking to you every day,
acquainting you with what you
didn't know,
          hadn't heard of   before.
You threw my words out.
          Rejected
like an old rug that's of no use no more.
The voices grew strong, taking over
and you believed.
          One day they moved in
          while I was away and refused
to leave,
growing stronger
by the minute as you sat
          helpless
and listened to their
chatter like a spool unwound.
When will this end and you return
          to me, or is that not willed, something
we cannot talk about anymore?
I am here now,
          flung away in the corner,
          unwanted,
but waiting, helpless as your fears rise
and the voices take over
          completely.

Fantasy

Are we meant to spend
the rest of our lives only looking
at each other across
an empty road?

Is there nothing else for us
in this short space of our
lives already made
shorter by the passing years?

Is this all?
Is this enough?

To you it maybe all you want.
But for me it is mere crumbs off a plate and
I want more. Can we have a life together?
Will you come to me?
But how long should I wait?
I'm not getting any younger.
And neither are you.

Alone One Evening

The dog sang soprano,
her tone melodious.
She had lost her way to the stage,

but that didn't matter.
Her voice
was still intact.

She sang of friends
long gone, of days past
and memories remembered.

She sang of dreams dreamt during
the day, of faraway places
only she knew.

She sang in high pitch, and from
somewhere down the road a
tenor rang out loud and clear.

Walk Away

You took my life from me.

Yet it was not yours to acquire.

I was a mere whisper in
the dark recesses
of the room
that you plucked out of
the shadows at will

like you always do, killing
the fire within.

The look in your eyes
told me things I'd seen before and
I rose to run away, but

my feet were bound to
the floor.
I could not move and you walked all
over me, again.

The firefly flashed
its laughter at my inability
to move, to defend my right.

Yet what was I to defend?

I was a mere
crumpled whisper that
no one heard.

Accountable to No One

I'm not the doormat you
wipe your feet on
returning home from work, the dirt
of the city smeared
across my cheek again,
walk over, all over shedding
morsels of the places you have roamed.

I'm not your tablemat to
eat off, place your plate piled
with a mountain of food for
your sustenance
whenever you think it is required.

I'm not your prayer mat you
prostrate on
extending arms forward, your back
a globe
raised to the heavens
supplicating in front of an
invisible God asking
for everything you desire, but
cannot be given.

There's only so much one can get and
however much asking and pleading
will not be of use, although you
think otherwise
as actions articulate your folly.

I'm not a placemat for
your coffee mug, a bedside mat to
warm your feet when you
get up on a cold morning, your ugly
toes smelling of stale sweat, or,
a wall-to-wall carpet
you can sprawl on, move
from side to side like a
stray dog that's
glad to have found a home.

There is a difference.
I'm me.

Not like the rest that lets
you get away with it all and hold
their heads in silence, tongues zipped up,
thoughts thrown deep into the back of
an almirah, because
they have no
choice but accept your ways.

The Woman in the Picture

He wanted your breasts
thrusting out from the screen.
Creamy white with pink tips like some
exotic sweet he could never taste.
Denied.
His desire rose.
Twin towers,
they brought them down a long time ago.
Twin peaks stare at him, bold and defiant.
He stared back,
but the words scribbled in the valley between
stirred his anger.
A cleavage
full of Arabic dissent.

You would be punished for your insolence,
for daring to bare it all for the world
to see and read.
Think thoughts they shouldn't for someone
else's woman. He would destroy those peaks.
Eighty lashes and stoning to death to
teach you a lesson in subjugation.
Don't mess with desires he kept
hidden away, don't make him yearn
for things he couldn't have.

But your family feared his words
and whisked you away.
Said you were mad, not quite right.
Imprisoned within high walls they stuff
pills and lies to make you forget.
Fire and ice, but your mind
screams out to frolic with
the wind lashing at the walls outside.

The Decision

I worry that you might not like this,
but we continue anyway.
The wine tastes sour like grapes you bought
the other day, but refused to eat
because you didn't like the color.
They tasted alright to me,
sweet with a hint of sour that is what I've
come to expect of grapes, and of this thing
we call a relationship.

You drink coconut oil because
someone sent you a story that people
were guzzling it in America.
Your brain needed it, you said.
Anything American was fine with you.
If they thought it right to swallow
coconut oil then who were you to complain?
I hid a smile, but you saw it
and were annoyed.
We've been cooking with it for years, so
why the sudden need to drink it like water?

You shrugged and tried to convince me,
like you did that time with the reason why
crocodiles sit with their mouths open.
They want to catch butterflies,
you said, while I laughed till my sides
cracked and the tears
coursed down my cheeks.

Now the tears trickle for a different reason,
but you don't see them anymore.
You have lost your way to over here, or
perhaps you pretend as you think it best.

In Search of a Man

Of all the men there are only
a few of marriageable value.

Approximately thirty percent are already
married, happily or unhappily, I don't care.

Twenty percent are gay and
content to be that way.

That leaves fifty. Of this,

twenty five percent are terrorists, thugs,
fundamentalists, jihadist, women beaters,
pedophiles and other undesirables
no one in their right mind would even
consider for anything.

Except if you want to become
a politician.

Then the underworld connection
comes in handy. Along with the undesirables.

But since politicians are mostly men
themselves, they won't really
need to marry into the underworld.
Or an undesirable for that matter.

Back to the equation.

Ten percent are sitting on the fence
trying to figure out if they
want to be gay or happy.

They are the fool's best friends.
No one can help them.
Not the straight.
Not the gay.
Not even the politicians.

The balance fifteen percent are
made up of ten percent of men who
can be married. But.

And here's the real crux.
Five percent are in the process of
getting married, and it would be
a shame to pull them apart.

Five percent are waiting to see how much
dowry they can get in return for nothing else
except their maleness,
which is really insignificant.
But you won't have their mothers say that.

The only sane five percent that's
any good getting married to
has everyone queuing up for them
like they do in front of an embassy for a visa.

I really can't be standing
in a queue for anything let alone a man.
So I'd rather be single with
no hang-ups attached.
Don't want to be like my friend
who married a "nice" man,
only to find he had
someone stashed up inside his closet.
And there began the sham.

In Control

He pulled open the doors and ripped out
the seams. The curtain crashed
to the ground as she screamed.

He laughed as he usually did
in moments like this.
The thing was sharp; it always made its mark.
Sport for him, it was such unending pleasure.

Not for her.

She could sit back and enjoy with him, if
she chose, but she did not, preferring instead
to make those ugly sounds.
Those sounds he hated so much.
"No," she screamed over and over and over
in her little voice that was all she had.
He hated the sound.
Why did she have to hurt him so?
The noise grated in his ear.
So mournful. So unwelcome.

"No."
There it was again.
"Shut up!" he screamed in annoyance and
thrust deep inside.
They were all the same, shouting the same
thing.
"No."

It sounded like a dirge.

It made the whole experience dirty, ugly, like
something that was not quite right.

Something he wasn't supposed to have.
And he didn't like that. He wanted it all.
Always wanted,
but why didn't they stop?
He took the thing
out, now bloodied and dirty,
and cursed her lying there in sobs.

You Can't Handle It

We've got brains, little gray cells
bubbling with enthusiasm,
intelligence that astounds leaving you
gaping like a fool.
Knowledge beyond your wildest imagination.

We come on strong, rule the world if
we want to. Prime Ministers
and Presidents—we've made it to the top.
Astronauts, doctors, lawyers,
musicians, singers, writers, poets and
dreamers; movers and shakers.

But you can't handle it.

You bring in rules to put
us down, make us slaves to your wishes
that prop you up, call us names, tag us
with insults. The weaker sex,
you smirk.

Because you can't handle it.

No you can't. We've got class, we've got
style, we've got a whole lot of vitality.
We strut our stuff around
the world, drive you wild with desires
you dare not name.

But you can't handle it.

You postulate religious decrees,
some God said it's so.
You pick up an old book and hide
behind a God you created in your own image.
No woman here, not even to give birth.
And you declare that God said
obey the man even though he is weak,
has no control over his thoughts,
his words, his actions, the way his tongue flaps
aimlessly like an old rag left
on the clothes line.
You convey a multitude of reasons for your
arguments, divine interventions
to prove your point. But

we know you can't handle it.

We stand up strong.

You rape and torture and
target us even when small and unable
to defend ourselves against brute force.

You forget we have rights too.
Law enforcement men turn the other way or
tell us we deserved it for being who we are.
They hurt us more, but we stand our ground.

You force us inside homes,
tell us it's our place, to keep the
home fires burning while you
roam the streets, an ancient tradition that
you created to keep us safe, throw shrouds
over us and tell us God willed it so.
Hide behind the hood, cover your eyes,
your brains, your ears, don't tempt the man,
who's weak and getting weaker.

You can't handle it.

We rise up in crowds, a million voices
across the world from
villages and towns, cities and foreign lands,
our names you can't even pronounce.
We are one half of the world you try to hide.

You are afraid of our power, of what we can do.
So you ban our marches, protests, send police
in riot gear, tear gas to disperse,

because, you simply can't handle it.

We give birth, we bring forth life,
we hold your destiny in the palm of our hands.
One move, a blink of the eye and
we can get rid of what we create.
Treat us well for we decide
who lives and who rots inside the womb.
Born of a woman you should think twice if it's
right to treat us so.

You can't handle it,

we know you can't even fathom where to start.
But your words can't admit that,
to do so would be defeat and you can't
handle bowing down to
a woman, now can you?

Inside the Old Room

What would the walls say if only
they could speak?
Would they
tell you of the fantasies I dream
when I am not with you?
Or my thoughts I speak out
for no one to hear
lest hearing make real?
What would they say, those walls,
if they could converse with
you and me?

Would they ask me
to leave for daring to do
that which I should not?
For I am a mere thing to please.
Nothing more to you.

On the Cheap Side of Town

Foundation cream works, sometimes,
but it can't hide the bruises on
her cheek or cover the
dark circle under the eye, someone's gift
to her for not doing as he wished.

She winces
remembering the pain, hearing
words yelled as he came at her and the slap
on her face resounding like an
echo in her mind rolling over like thunder.

She smiles at her reflection staring back,
a gaunt face sunken eyes; dead inside,
no longer holding her smile,
warm and inviting.
Teenage innocence lost in a night.

Everything has changed.
She's all grown up.

Dark kohl frames her eyes, mascara
helps hide the pain.
Bright red on lips to entice.
She sighs softly. It's just a job, she
whispers to herself.
Just a job.

A small room in the city, a few scraps
to keep the hunger at bay, the rest
sent back to a home
in the village where they wait.
There's nothing there for anyone.
No land to work on, a small house

and many mouths to feed.
She's ready for the show.
Long hair straightened last month
caresses shoulders, unlike hands that wait
to claw her clothes off later on,
trying to gain pleasure inside a
cheap hotel room or the back of a car.
Old shoes, the heels torn, pasted
over hurriedly not to notice.

It's a game she took on to save the rest.
She remembers the home she will
never visit for the shame
she carries inside her heart, blinks back tears
threatening to pour out.

It's a job like any
other, peddling
her wares is the price she pays.
She paints her face to hide her pride
and take on the game on the street.

Sadness

You killed me with your
words yesterday, but I did not die;
not like you thought I would.

I sat there for a while then
rose and left, quietly, shutting
the door behind as I
slipped out. Silent
in my own little world,

a piece inside smashed into
smithereens, pierced by your words
as I walked away. Forever.

Response to a Man

You can't mold me into
something you want—those
rough hands trying to create
dreams that can only shatter.
You are no sculptor and cannot shape
perfection from mud nor
chisel beauty out of a slab of granite.
I am flesh and blood
just like you.
Not made of clay or rubber that
bends at your will.
Don't even try to change me
for you will not like the person
I might become in your hands.
Leave me as I am and let me
mold myself as I have done all this while.
I am an individual, a human.
Not a doll made of plastic
or wood that you take out to play
when it pleases you.

Fault Lines

The lines on my hand
recount a story I can't hide from you.

Sita stepped over the line.

Fortune visits those blessed to
lead the kind of life they desire.
She didn't want to be restricted.

My life stretches before me a
long and winding road that
meanders through emerald
woods, ascends cliffs and floats
along streams rushing to wherever.
Fate intersects,
but I stand strong.
*She was fed up, not
what she had agreed when they met.
Who was to say
the lines weren't drawn to wander
on her palms?
Maybe they read it
and remained silent because they
couldn't change destiny.*

*She was a woman
and had to be confined.*

My lines travel the world, crisscross
continents,
scale mountains
to lose themselves in valleys deep.

*She stepped out for
some fresh air.*
I reap my own rewards.
*She
was looking for adventure, a new life.*
I pick
my path even if it is
wrought with fear and pain. Striding
with head held up, high heels
tapping my beat
to melodies only I want to sing.
*What stood in front of her
was better than what she was
leaving behind.*
I had an education, a job,
money at hand. I could do as I pleased.

*They changed
the story. Said he
abducted her.*
Said

she was

out

of

line.

I didn't want him, ineffective.

He would bring me down to his level, a
worm slithering in the
damp undergrowth afraid
of the light.
Her strength.
His weakness to protect her.
I sent him away. I could do better
than that.

His shame took kingdoms to war.
Millions died, but those lives didn't
matter; non essentials, expendable.

I refused to answer his call.
He pleaded
     like

          an
          ant.
                    He dragged her
            back, his trophy, his possession.
               She insulted his authority.

I'm no one's
treasure. Not a prize won at
a game not a plaque to
hang
on
the wall.
            She wanted something more
            than what she was getting.

I concur. Totally agree.
            She was condemned.
I have an option.

            She wasn't given her preference.
     She walked into flames, red hot she
     rose. They still wonder.
            Can't make up their minds.
     Can't call him
            a fool. Not after so long.
The narrative remains the way he wrote it.

They look on silently at my attempts
to rule my universe.
I stand strong.

The Relationship

She went into the garden
to pick a flower.

She smelt it
plucked out the scent, sent it flying
on the wind to the other side of the world.
Petals wilted, cowering,
doors closed, an aged being.

She crushed it between her fingers
tight. Not even a thin line to escape.
Pondering the moment, feeling
the limpness within, she
opened her hand, threw the flower
in the drain.

That about summed their relationship.
A beginning, middle and
an end. Amen.

Asking for It

They say I'm
asking for it because they
don't like the clothes I wear, want to
put me in a shroud. Yet the picture
on the net someone posted
the other day says it all—the man groping
a woman in a burqa, all covered up
like a big black garbage bag,
nothing showing, not even the eyes. But no.

I'm wrong.
I'm a woman.
I should know better.

Dress decently. Whatever that means.
Don't show your arms, your legs, your midriff.
Your neckline's too low, the eyes
wander down the road, the T-shirt
too tight, your breasts pop out.
Don't you realize
they are meant to stand up strong
not flop down like a lonely phallus stuck tight
between your legs?

Do you realize those words thrown at me
don't make sense? Don't wear jeans, it's not
in our culture, we are conservative, Asian,
jeans — foreign. They are too tight,
they excite men when you move.
Don't roll your hips when you walk, you
are tempting them, merely by
walking from here to there.

Don't go out late at night.
You are asking for it.

Don't wear those clothes that
stick to your body like another skin, you
can't blame him if he does
something he's not supposed to, like rape you,
behind a dumpster, or somewhere
less conspicuous. That's not his fault.
It was you.
All you. You were inviting him, remember.

You look at me and decide for yourself
even before I've opened my mouth
to tell you anything.
The way I dress seems to say
consent to you to do what you want.
A fleeting look your way and you get
all excited, I led you on by giving you the look,
when I only glanced your way to check
if you were about to attack me, as I felt your
ugly stares running all over my body
like you were undressing me.

Don't cross your legs,
it turns them on,
you are soliciting it. Leave your legs
where they are, preferably at home,
with the rest of you. That would be best
because he needs to go someplace
and you are distracting him,
making him want to do things he
wouldn't dream of if you weren't there.
He's such a good man. A model citizen.
It was just that you
were asking for it.

In the House No One Visits

Why am I waiting
when everything around
is falling apart?
The door bangs shut, loud
and hard, closing out the world
to me as I
sit alone waiting. There's no
reason for me to remain
by myself in
this room,
this house, that you call a life.
Not mine, but all yours.

Always yours.

I speak in whispers lest it reach your
ears and hurt you to the point
you hurt me back. In return.
Like a gift, always given. Never asked for.
Yet I don't want your gifts
of hurt, pain and hate. I want
none of the things you
think I want - jewelry, fancy clothes that
don't suit me - except
my life back as it was.

Before you took it away to play.

The End

Your sentences flew in
the air, birds terrified by the sudden gunfire
in the distance wondering if
it would reach them. They hover uncertain
for a moment to settle slowly
on the ground.
I pick them up
one by one, wipe off the dust.

You flung them at me in a fit of rage,
thunder cracking above as you
walked out the door slamming it shut.
Finality.
Outside the rain crashes on the roof, winds
howl and branches of trees crack in
agony, but you don't care.
It drenches you
in seconds, your clothes clinging in fear
like a dog that doesn't want to be alone.

You don't bother to stop.
Or wait until the world has changed its mood.
You need to get out,
move away, far, far away, do anything but
be here where I am. I stare as you
walk through the thick
sheet of rain and disappear around the corner.
Lost. The rain plunges blinding
my view, drowning my muffled sobs
with its roar of disapproval. Turning
around I pick up the broken pieces that's all
you left me, pour them into a jar
for safe keeping.

Saturday Afternoon

It was supposed to be their
wedding today.

The celebrations would have started;
flowers, candles, cake, and she,
dressed as a bride. But

she's sitting here
in her old jeans and T-shirt
looking out the window at clouds bolting
as if in a hurry to get to some
other festivity that she's not invited to.

Birds sing in the trees reminding her
of the band that would have played.

It's an auspicious day; the stars are placed
right where they should be, blinking
their blessing on her.
And him.

They would have been rejoicing, smiling
and laughing, but when it was time
to send the invitations he changed his mind.
Refused her calls, couldn't bear to explain.

"Don't make a fuss," he warned when she
demanded he see her one last time.
"I don't want a scene."

The place he chose couldn't have been
more public.
What did he expect?
That she would run across
the keys of the grand piano
in the hotel lobby playing tunes with her toes,
roll on the floor crying out for him,
stomp on tables and scream out his name
like she was calling out
to God, or swing from the chandelier
while people snapped it up on
camera phones to post on Instagram?

She left the ring he gave on the table
in front of him and
walked out
with no second glance,
hiding tears spilling from
her eyes, no words exchanged.

What else was she to do?

Market in Peshawar

In a small shop hidden between
many others he opened up a trunk
and showed me
the spoils of a civilization felled by religion
the previous day.

The head of the ruler hung in public display
in the heart of town, rotting in the sun.
No proper burial for him they condemned.

Dogs stared up, sniffed at the legs sticking
down, but didn't bark for fear of
being treated the same.

Men silenced in shock, women and girls
too young to understand
forced inside homes pock marked with bullets,
roofs opened up to let in the elements
as winter moved in stealthily.

Old silver, dulled by the years
of constant use, heavy in my hand.
I picked up a bracelet narrow and long.
It fitted like a glove.
Decorated metal handcuffs
adorned my arms glinting in the light filtering
in through a slit in the curtains.

What petite hands owned these pieces?
Was it someone like me with wrists
so small a narrow barrel of decorated silver
could slip over them
with ease sans a key to fling it open?
Was it child or woman?

Did she look like me?
I wondered as I stared at my arms,
brown, adorned with silver
grown lackluster by the sands of time,
buried, perhaps for safety in some
old chest or almirah, wrapped in cloth so
no one could guess.

Who found them lying there amidst
the rubble of a house once well preserved?

Did she know her treasures were gone,
snatched by someone in search of
wares to peddle, or did she give them to him
sitting in front of me,
pleading for a few coins to fill her stomach,
buy a ticket to somewhere safe?

He didn't understand my questions, or
maybe he pretended he didn't.
It was better this way for all, it seemed.
Knowledge is power and it can destroy.
She lived,
perhaps in a better place, who was to know
for sure, while he sold her history
and I bought.

Two bracelets sit side by side inside
my clothes cupboard as I recollect that day
a long time ago, far away,
in a distant place I would never visit
for fear of religious fury unleashed on
the likes of me that refuse to conform.
The silver stares and tries
to tell me stories of its past, but I can't
understand the language it speaks.

Flowers chiseled in deep, little open spaces
like windows to let in the light,
a lock that is stuck with no key, lost
in the haste to flee.
The answers remain over there,
somewhere,
hidden inside a shop on the streets of
Peshawar with a man, now
grown old, who guards it well.

The Man from Over There

I found a verse I wrote to you
a long time ago.
It was sitting on top of an old paper
torn from the exercise book.
The scribbles in pencil, fading in time
and would have disappeared
if I hadn't looked inside the trunk
full of old things.
There it sat waiting for over a decade.
Waiting to be rescued and put down
on new paper where it could
breathe in fresh breezes and not be
confined to the stale dry air
of the old trunk.

The verse about you
described you as you were. As you are.
Nothing seems to have changed.
You should have changed.
Grown wiser, better,
but you have not.
And as I read my verse about you
written so long ago I recognized
you as you are.
As you were.
As you will become.
Nothing has changed with you.
While I soar above it all, a better person.
But you wouldn't know.
Your brain does
not have the capacity to know.
If it did you will change too, now,
wouldn't you?

Memories

Your desire
entwines me, swathes me in an embrace
like the soft silk saree I
bought from the looms of Benares
many years ago.
Gossamer weave I feel
the delicate touch caress
my skin, the subtle fingers of a feather
fallen off the back of a dove, unnoticed.
Muted hues of earthy red
run through in patterns etched in gold
like veins in my body
you try to control.
Rivers of hope run on, henna
green leaves block printed
by the hands of man in strange designs
like the words you murmur in my
ear or the faint touch of
breath on my shoulder. Your voice trails
with stories of a past I
can't hold onto,
yet I try, wrapping myself in the folds
of fabric as it twists and turns
making bold statements to cascade across
my shoulder like a limp rag,
now falling flat, now billowing out
and fluttering in the breeze as I
stretch my arms to fold you in.
Desire spent,
we lie in silk
as memories flood in.

On a Hot Afternoon

Thirty times I checked
my phone today, but nothing, nothing.

The screen beams back its usual face.
Not a message or a missed call
to indicate you care. The day meanders.

Coconut branches outside my room sway
in amusement at my distress.
"He's not called yet,"
they whisper on the wind.
"Not called yet, not called yet, not called yet."

Birds take up the chant flying
to the neighbors garden, the next town and
beyond. Butterflies wander in silence.

You couldn't be with a poet,
too cramped, too strange.
You didn't understand what I wrote.
The words were not right.

You found comfort in numbers
and straight roads.
The bottles lined up on the table in single file
while I lived in a world you couldn't enter, or
so you said. We were universes apart,
my ideas contrasting, mixing and merging,
colors on a painters palette.
My mind was my own, not a toy you could
play with or mold to your desires.

You couldn't accept that.
Was that why you didn't call?

Lines of Control

Refusing to be confined by
an invisible line, she crossed over to
the other side.
Oh the pleasure of decision making,
empowering for a woman forced
inside a house
detained in
an indiscernible circle drawn
by a man who had no respect for women.
Why else would he chop off
her nose and bring forth the wrath of
her brother?
She had enough of these fools that
called themselves men.
She reached the end of her tether
and wanted out. He was waiting
with his plane.
A flight plan already mapped out.
She was free, but only for a few blissful days.
He came to collect his looted treasure.

Another century
another place
she was acquired again, and again
the owner marched in to seize control.

Wars were fought.
Sita and Helen they both
wanted out,
out of the unpleasantness they were forced
to lead that wasn't life, but
paid the ultimate price
for freedom and love.

Independence demanded
the ultimatum—she walked through fire,
but it wasn't enough. He threw her away.
She grew old with despair.
Too many lives lost in vain.
The thousand ships sailed away.

Draupadi was pawned in a game of dice.
Srija was left in the drain.
Nirbhaya torn apart
and thrown out like trash.
Someone with a forgotten name was sacrificed
on the altar of commerce.
Little girls from a poor country sold as slaves.
Their bodies could warm gnarled old men.
Innocence stolen for adult pleasures.
Money spoke, eloquent like wine.
Children, always the children
forced to pay.

Everyday someone was ground in the dust.

The hands of the woman holding the scales
trembled with fury at the injustice,
but no one could take off the blindfold.

Aphrodite stood helpless to defend
without her arms.
But arms can do only so much.

The lines kept getting longer.
No one cared.

Remember how Magdalene
was condemned by
the old men seeking to make a
name for themselves?

Couldn't bear the thought that she
was better, more intelligent than they were,
or that she was the chosen one
from all his crowd.
A woman selected to carry on his message.
How could that be?

Joan's voices were damning the men
they didn't like the attention
she was getting.
Too much publicity for a mere village girl.
She had the Dauphin in her hand.
They wanted him dancing to their tune.
She thwarted their plans.
The stakes were too high. She had to go.
No one survives a fire.
It was easier to call her a witch,
dangerous,
might do strange things to the children.

They were out of line,
all of them. Had to be brought under control.
Of the men.

Delhi News

The newspapers said it was
suicide; that he hung himself in the cell.
Pressure kicked in.
Ugly expressions all around, unfriendly
comments drumming into his ears.
He began to see it was wrong,
what he did to her that day in the dark
with his friends by his side. Shame, remorse;
but too late. No one wanted to know.
It sounded like a joke.

He decided to leave it to God.
He looked up and saw the rope
waiting for him.
Beckoning.

His family was aghast.
They think he got some help.
After all,
everyone knew he was a coward.
The incident on the bus proved it.
But no one's interested in their theories.

There are other more
important things to talk about, like
the cost of living or
injustice in another country. Anything to turn
the attention away from reality.

Questions Left Unanswered

A head in the drain, he
tried to understand why.

They took him in for questioning,
dragging him out of the house.

A rude awakening.

Fifteen years of sharing life,
but can you really know someone?

He thought he did

until they told him about the head,
bloodied and severed
from the impact, lying in the drain
and the many lives lost on the street.

She stopped the rush hour traffic
with her swift movements.
Nothing remained
except pieces of lives swimming
on the street and soaking into the earth
to disappear the next day.
The numbers
could only be imagined.

The hole in the ground,
smoke on the air and the smell
of burning, burning.

He sits in the front room
of the house they once shared
unable to go inside as the memories
have shattered into tiny fragments.
They lie scattered across the floor
like the flowers of the Sepalika tree in
the early morning dew.
He wonders at it all, trying to understand,
while in the jungles
far away,
someone else is groomed,
to take her place.

Trapped

The lightness of her step
faltered—it trembled in shock,
the incident went unnoticed—the day
a tent settled over her head,
billowing like a cloud
floating, snuffing out the sun, long hair
flattened against her head.
Sky blue, light weight covering her all around,
a lace grill to hide her eyes.

It was hard to walk, place her feet
one in front of the other, slowly, surely,
stumbling over stones, wading
through potholes under the swirling blue.
Smothered under a heaving wave,
thrashing to stay afloat.
Found it hard to move, get about
on the street accompanied by a man walking
a step ahead. Always ahead.
Master of her universe.

Found it hard to dance.
To play the fool.
Taboo.

She wilted inside, a flower all dried up, a
desert rose that never bloomed, no
sustenance, fresh air, no
underwater gurgling streams, no
sun playing on her face.

No one saw, no one cared.
She was just another blue speck
on the harsh landscape. This was her life.

They told her it was willed that way.
That was the right way.
To be hidden from sight, not a person.
A mere thing to please.
A slave in the house not even hers,
cooking, cleaning, taking care of him, the
old gnarled man like the tree outside
waiting, waiting to fall down tired out, no
life left, hobbling along.
Veins dried up, lines crisscrossing
over and over.
A baby mill made to produce at his command.
They all said that was the way it was willed,
written down, memorized, called out
five times a day and after a while she

began to believe.
Began to accept her lack of choice,
her lips sealed by invisible tape.

But the little voice hiding inside,
the one they forgot to pull out,
the one that secreted itself
behind the door, screamed in protest.
It howled in agony and beat its head against
blue walls trying to get out.
"Let me out, let me be."
No one hears cries through walls of fabric.
No one cares about what happens
Inside blue rooms.
She blocked out the little voice
with loud prayer and the darkness swirled in
taking over her thoughts, descending
to murky depths.

Control

He tells me my hair
isn't right, straighten it,
that's the fashion.
When I do, he's not satisfied.

Rain never falls in straight lines, there are
always breaks, pauses between raindrops
like hyphens tumbling from the sky.

He tells me my hair's
too short, grow it long and thick, tie it back
in a braid to fall along the
contours of my spine.
Women should not look like men.
They should wear their hair at
a certain length.

He takes pains to point out
all that's wrong with my clothes,
the hemlines unfashionably long, my arms
all covered up.
Why am I so conservative?
He laughs, as if that's something wrong.
Wear shorts, tank tops,
he wants to see my legs and arms,
don't I feel warm?

He tells me my blouse is too revealing,
everything is exposed,
aren't I ashamed to be seen like that?
Cover up,
that's not the way women in
our society dress.

Don't wear makeup,
don't use those strange colors.
My lips look bloodstained, and what's that
stuff on my eyes?

He tells me I'm wasting my time
sitting around doing nothing all day.
Get a job
go to an office
tire myself out so I won't have time
to do anything else, like
write or think for myself.

He tells me I'm
wasting my talents writing poems.
Go start a website, a news portal
like that person he knows.
Write about politics and world affairs.

But I do, I say, and show him a poem.
That's not politics.
He throws it away.
You are so talented, you have
such a good grasp of things.

That's why I write,
I whisper to the winds.

But poetry is
not for fools, stories can't convince clowns
hanging around for handouts — praise
from politicians and empty heads.

He tells me I should
change my name, try something else,
something modern, doesn't realize that
everything that made me
who I am, this person
standing in front of you took
a long time evolving and he wants to
remake me,
wants me to give up
being me
to become nothing.
Not even a whisper thrown to clouds,
a dream hidden inside an old trunk
that can be taken out
and believed in when no one's around.

He wants to transform me,
craft me into a lost soul straining
under a dark veil.
A form that's dead inside.

I'd rather he went
someplace else and let me be
who I am with my
unruly, curly, unmanageable hair,
my arms bare,
cocooned in my beliefs ancient as they are,
writing my lines to the world
that he doesn't understand
and my name—my name, you call out,
my name—inherited,
ancestral right,
my very own.

Making Up My Mind

I will not dress to please
except myself, for I'm my
own woman and you
have no voice to raise against
my wishes.
She that bends to your say is no different
from the branches that bend and sway
at the command of the tree or
the whim of the breeze
passing through.
I bend and break to no man's command or
any fools whim to be pleased.
I rise and fall in the tempestuous waves
of my own desires that leave
no room for fools to navigate.

Goddess in Chains

He's in charge of her every move,
all of her he owns.
Every action controlled
far better than
a performer in the circus
moving to the ringleader's whip crack.

He's there before she opens her eyes
brushes away the dreams she wants
to make real, but can't,

not anymore.

The faint light outside, the dog's low growl
in the distance as he undresses her
in the dark behind the velvet curtain,
gold, gaudy designs, her image
embroidered
sequins bedazzle.
Unravels the many yards of silk
from around her waist.

Yesterday's saree,
gold threads gleam in the soft light, rustle
of silk fall at her feet.

Was he reminded of Draupadi?

Rough hands, clumsy caress.
Water poured from tiny goblet trickles
at his feet. Soft splashes,
washes away the night sweat.
A new saree pulled out, in shades
he chooses,

not what she wants.
Carefully pleated,
pinned,
eyes averted
from her ample bosom, she cringes in shame.
He thinks she blushes for him
smiling a slow, knowing smile
as she bites her lip.
The same place every day.

New clothes wrapped around her body
heavy jewelry round her neck, garlands
of fresh jasmine from the woman
near the gate,
wound by stained, old fingers
in the early morning, marigold
from the gardens beyond.
Oil lamps lit outside, sweet perfume from
incense fills the room, the smoke
fashions another veil across her face.

She's ready for the day.

He leaves her behind the curtain
to wait for his command while
crowds gather
straining for a view through the door.

He acquaints her with
what to do, whom to bless.

Keeps her awake when
all she wants is to shut her eyes and let
herself drift to places she would rather be,
instead of there,
cooped up inside a small space.

Four walls, claustrophobic, smell of the heat,
sweaty bodies coming for favors.
No windows for winds to rush in, the
only space at the door,
constantly blocked.

He sings her praise, extols her attributes,
calls out the many, myriad names he has
given her,
not hers, never hers.

He feeds her throughout the day.
Places trays of fruit
at her feet; stinking, overripe that she
all but gags on.
It's what he thinks fit for her, what
she should consume not what she wants.
Who's to say she only eats fruit?
Never asks if she prefers biriyani instead.
Rice and curry with pol sambol and kiri kos or
hot and spicy noodle soup.
Chocolate cake with cream
oozing from the layers when bitten into.

He shuts her in at
his convenience.

Speaking through her tongue
uttering words she would never say, teasing
her disciples with strange pronouncements
expecting her to perform miracles,
stuck inside a stone image.

A puppet in a show, she's hidden
behind a veil of lies.
He controls the crowds
with a pat on their heads, blessings
through peacock feathers from
someone else's ride.
More flowers, wishes, and endless
pleas and requests for
worldly desires.

Pattini, Durga, Saraswathy,
Badrakali, Lakshmi,
dancing to his tune.
Goddesses all, invisibly chained.
Kali, you too, stepping to his beat.
Immortal souls imprisoned
by man, doing as he wants.
Caught in a cycle of deception, Goddesses
hard at work selling their wares
to the highest bidder.
The pimp calls the numbers.
She's forced to perform. Rules have changed.

Goddesses in chains.
Smiles don't reach inside.
The faces are the same.
None of them free, no longer in control.
Dancing to the man's command.

On Campus: Just Before the Exam

Blade glistening silver
in sunlight. *in out in out*
Did you see it shine,
the knife in his hand?   *in out in out*

What did it look like as he
pulled it out?   *in out in out*
Out of its sheath of last
week's newspaper
old with use, picked up from the kitchen
or was it sparkling new, bought
a few days ago
just for the occasion,
especially for you? *in out in out*

You.
The woman of his dreams.
You. The woman who
unmade him. You.

Did he tell you where he got it
or was there no time as he thrust it in deep?
in out in out
Did you think he'd go through,
the coward he was?   *in out in out*
Who'd have thought it could do
so much?   *in out in out*
Blood spurting a fountain
in the middle of the road. *in out in out*

The asphalt changed color   *in out in out*
mixing and merging   *in out in out*
red carpet covering, sticky and new.
Did you feel it tearing you up? *in out in out*

Thirty five times.   *in out in out*
In the valley of your breasts.   *in out in out*
At the apex of your legs.   *in out in out*
You turned to run get away, disappear
be somewhere else, move as
fast as you can.   *in out in out*

He pulled you close by your thick long hair.
Hair he loved to run his fingers through.
          in out in out,
a rope snaking behind,
trying to slither away to someplace safe.
in out in out

Did he think he was in a movie,
acting the lover?   *in out in out*
Flirting between trees?   *in out in out*
Soft music playing in the background wafting
towards him.

Stabbed in the back you
heard it go in.   *in out in out*
Deep inside you felt it cut through.
He wouldn't stop,
          not a moment to rest,   *in out in out*
he worked in frenzy *in out in out*
all that rage,
all those years,   *in out in out*
the pain of rejection.   *in out in out*

Your steps faltered, you fell.   *in out in out*
Oozing like a can of juice. *in out in out*
Thirty five places, thirty five cuts,
for the liquid to flow,   *in out in out*
flow, while they stood and watched
his friends, at a distance *in out in out*
hovering like storm clouds   *in out in out*

98

growling overhead *in out in out*
but refusing to move in.

He pulled out a vial.   *in out in out*
The jilted lover.   *in out in out*
Oh what sorrow, wronged, helpless,
such sweet, sweet sorrow. *in out in out*
The lid twisted open it reached his lips
        in out in out
but his friends rushed to the rescue.
How could he think of it?
He had his whole life ahead, so much
potential, so much to live for.

They dashed in to save him   *in out in out*
pulled the bottle from his hands *in out in out*
took away the knife
threw away the evidence.
Then they all fled.   *in out in out*
They moved as one.
They ran away

She remained where she fell   *in out in out*
sprawled at the side of the road, on
the way to the classroom.   *in out in out*
There was no one to care.
No one to pick her up.
No one to take her side.   *in out in out*
She remained.
        She bled.   *in out in out*
He fled.   *in out in out*
        She died.   *in out in out*
        He lived.   *in out in out*
He lived.

He lives.

He Wanted too Much

Dreaming of mining for rubies
at the higher reaches of my legs,
climbing up, up, up,
like a mountaineer ascending Annapurna.
You seek pearls glistening white
like the day they were prised
from bellies of oysters in the deep.
A cave deep and dark, portal to the truth you
seek everywhere, but don't find.
Love's an illusion you cannot hold or
holding, find hard to contain, for
what you seek is not love, but things you
aren't allowed to have, like half sentences
mumbled in communal beds,
avoiding eyes that find it hard to lie.
Yet you come to me
pleading for the one thing barred from you,
for you don't understand
the depth of my being.
You are too much a fool for that.
I will not give to strangers
the right to mine what is mine,
and you have no voice
to raise on that.

Games People Play

Staring at the kettle, steam rising
to the ceiling, she's sitting in the kitchen in

her little house in London, wondering
what he's doing
so far away from home.

Sun's setting; she lounges
in the verandah in Colombo,

unsure when he'll leave. Colors change in
the garden, mango leaves turn golden.
She looks at him.

Shadows fall, walls whisper secrets.
"Doesn't know what he wants,
doesn't know what he wants."
Pink oleander strains
over the wall from the neighbors' garden.
Nods at him sitting silent
wondering what to do.

Messages whispered over phone lines,
crumpled in colored papers
thrown into dustbins.
Needs more time to decide.

Winter in London,
cold and chill like lilies
adorning a wreath.

A strange look in her
eyes, questions demanding to tumble out.
She doesn't say a word, but comes to him.
Sweating it out in the late afternoon heat her
blouse sticking to her like
a second skin.

Rising from her corner
she pours herself a coffee, staring at the rain
falling, falling through the trees.

He pulls her close to him, desires take over.
The game moves on, decisions
fly in the winds.

Silent Longing

I talk to the moon every night, but
she has stopped answering.

Sometimes during the afternoon
she comes out of hiding, tries to
get my attention
in a blue sky devoid of clouds to distract.

I know she hangs back in the firmament
after hours to think out a response
for me, but when it comes time to speak
her silence thunders across the dome.

She's been quiet since the day it happened.
She observed you walk in to my life
that murky day, make your way towards me.
The brightness was snuffed out as she
hid herself in shame.

All the stars in the heavens could have crashed
down to earth in protest at what you did.
But no one could compose
the tiniest sentence of disapproval.
There were no expressions
to describe your actions.

She's still trying to advise, let me know
I should get rid of you, but like me
her voice doesn't work when it's about you.

Why can't we speak up?
How did you take control over us both?
Our right to be heard?

I'm still waiting for the words to tell you
to go away while outside
the birds have brought their songs to a
standstill wondering if they should teach me
some of their words.

But they too are in shock,
for their language doesn't have
the terminology to describe what you do.

And the moon has swathed her face with
a cloud refusing to get involved.

Ganga

Sometimes she can't smell what's
right at her nose, the gaps in her senses
getting longer each time like
deepening shadows at dusk.
Sometimes she can't trace items
though they are in front
of her, she hunts, sniffs hard trying to locate
tiny drops of scents of familiarity hidden
behind cloud curtains in the mind.

Sometimes an image doesn't register,
but kindness remains,
she recalls with a wag of tail
acknowledges slowly what she would have
on earlier days been
quick to recognize, apologetic, a
strange look of puzzlement in her
eyes as if to say, did I
forget your face?

Sometimes she flops down, worn out
by supporting her weight, and waits patiently
for help, trusting someone will
find her at the edge of the garden unable
to move and lift her to her feet again.
Sometimes you
wonder if things could be reversed,

if a secret formula could transform,
take her down that narrow path back to
wherever, to whenever, before
it started to change
leaving fragments of
remembrance along the way.

But all roads to the past
seem to have been boarded up, weeds
grown across hiding the way, the flowers
withered and dried their fragrance no
longer pleasing.
Sometimes hope is all you have,
and the memories you
carry within.

Sometimes even that is lost.

To the Children Across Lines of Color and Race

Justice died the day
they tore her into little pieces, threw her
to winds howling a dirge
to the uncaring world, lifting shreds
one by one examining them—a hand
lost trying to cover eyes,
a teardrop balancing on a toe,
a finger pointing at the one advancing, and
a scream pushed back in a throat.

They scattered her
so far no one could unearth even
a speck, or
if finding, discover it hard to
piece together the story.

They stranded her at
the crossroads wondering what happened.

The sun climbs overhead to perch
on the centre of the dome. Birds sing softly
in trees hidden from view.
No one notices as leaves leave their
accustomed place on the branch
and flutter to the ground. They collect
on grass joining others already there
trying to lift themselves up
one last time, one last gasp of air,
to speak to the world before they
can move no more.

Another day, another time to mourn.

The sun slogs across the sky, slowly,
slowly it turns to night. Colors change, deep
amber, saffron and gold erased from view.
A black pall
falls into place as birds
take off on the wind in search of their homes,
a warm branch to rest weary heads
close their eyes and not bear witness to
things best left unsaid, until
the light shines once more.

Silence pervades a lonely world, yet
no one hears cries of
the fallen lying in dark places. Sobs of hurt,
bleeding, lost, incomprehension.
Muffled by a rough hand, threats
of punishments to befall.

The world moves on uncaring, while someone
picks up the old leaves and throws them
on the trash, no use to anyone anymore.

Earth Song

I am the weeping earth cringing
in pain when you dig me up, pulling out
limbs, entrails, leaving me to hemorrhage.
Shocked, in excruciating pain,
no one hears my silent cries.
Children orphaned, lives torn apart,
fracking my veins, drinking me dry.
Parched, I crumble into pieces.

I am the silent sky watching
anger whizz by to explode
in places you don't like.
Not yours to care while I listen to the
cries of the weak,
trying to make sense of it all
amidst terror raining down from above.

I am the roaring waves, the deep
darkness under heaving waters, flowing rivers,
gurgling streams, and silent lakes
that stand still as mirrors
for clouds to comb their hairs.
You dam me everywhere, but I
lift my head straining to rise,
course through the way I want, and not
how you think I should.

I am the raging fire that burns, taking
the trees with me chasing the birds away,
the deer, rabbits and wild beasts
that hide within my
voluminous cloaks.

Trees, how
I love to sway to bird's tunes,
the beat of squirrels feet,
weave my magic
through the land, burrowing in deep,
standing up tall, reaching high to
skies, waving
my many arms in the breeze, holding onto life.

I am woman, I am life,
I am earth, and I bleed.

In the Desert

How many stones does it take
to die?

Who will count the numbers picking up
each stone, one by one?
Will they be added up before and left
in little mounds, groups of ten, twenty or
more at the periphery of the grounds?

And will they then, after
the act takes place,
pick up the stones scattered around
and examine them?
See how many carry traces of blood,
morsels of brain, pieces of eye slithered out
in a vain attempt to hide,
and will they then decide
this was what it took to end it?

Will there be someone standing with a clock
timing every move, every sound, every cry,
taking notes, making comments
at the side of the page every time
a stone makes its mark?
And will he yell out in glee
when that takes place, just like the rest, or
will his lips remain sealed, the silent worker
performing his God given task to perfection?

And how will they know which
was the fatal blow?

Would her muffled cries have ceased
to rise on the wind, a terrified ant calling out
above the roar of the crowd raining down
like the monsoon in her home?
Would that be the sign or
would her head have stopped moving,
trying desperately to duck
after each blow as if to prevent
the next and the next and the next falling
down like confetti on her, stuck tight
inside a hole in the ground?

Would they stop sporting
at the end of an hour, or two, or three—when
every stone on the mounds have piled up in
a strange design around her head,
a halo of granite covering her from view, or
would they approach gleefully
pick up the stones for another round?

What do the stones look like?
Do they come in different shapes and sizes
with unusual hues against the grain?

Does someone go in search of them
to a specific place, a quarry
at the edge of town that
supplies them in abundance,
hold them in his palm, run his fingers
lovingly over the surface checking
for rough edges, the harder the better,
and who makes the final choice?

Who decides the rules of the game?

How many stones do you need
to kill a woman?
Is it the same amount needed to
kill a man, or is there a difference
in the sexes?
A mountain for a woman, a mere pebble
for a man?
Who makes the decisions?

It is all men.
Always the men.

Yet someone once said a long time ago,
he that casts a stone against another
should be
free from sin.

Not now,
not anymore.

Those words lost,
buried deep in the sands of time, to be
resurrected no more.

The End of Days

You cut and left me to die.
My arms hung aimless
fingers unfeeling, breezes halted above
refusing to wander through.
Fallen leaves caressed my skin
exposed to the world
making me wonder at what dark point
eyes must meet. Yet you avoided
turning your head my way.
Refused to look me in the eye, take
responsibility for what you did.

Rotten roots you said
as you dug in deep to pull out my history
leaving no trace to say who I was or
where I came from.

Earth gasped as you exhumed
my ancestral right, dragged out every
little piece left to remind the universe
about me. You felled me that day,
but did not think to ask if
it was ok. I have rights too, you know.
But all you did was laugh in
my face as I came crashing to the ground,
to rise no more.

Family Reunion

I am surrounded by
people who say I
need them all.
Yet I do not know them, those
people, strange faces, long names tripping
my tongue, shadows crawling
on the wall, hurrying across the ceiling
walking all over the place.
They force me to be
something else — a nobody,
an image like
the rest that nods at every word, flowers
to breezes wafting through.
They cramp my style. Fetter me in.
Teach me to be like them.
But I can't. Will not.
I protest to winds crashing
against trees and
thunder rolls in with a beat.
It amazes, saddens then
angers them that want me
caged like a parrot or some
strange bird bought from the shop to amuse.
But little do they realize I
came on my own – no
one to hold my hand and show me
the way, offer a ride in some
fancy car – and will leave unaccompanied too.
So why can't I live alone
without the confluence of the world
breaking my door to the ground?

The Poetess

She called herself a
poetess because she liked
the sound of it. Much better than
calling herself a teacher.
So plain, so common, so like
the girl next door.
But a poetess
could soar to places
no teacher could go.
So she told all she met she was a poetess.
A teacher too, but now
a poetess.

It was like graduating from
one level to the next.

The simple folks didn't understand.
They thought she had done something great.
She walked with a spring to her step.
Her expression serious. They turned around
as they saw her pass.
She felt such pride. At last to be known.
Even if to just a few.
They did not know she had
nothing to show.

A Princess Wronged

Easier for you,
flinging negative comments.

Making up stories, telling tales, dictating
the course of history the way you wanted.

They all believed the lie. I was ugly, you said.
Very ugly, you laughed to the trees
and the thunder grumbled, annoyed.
What difference did it make
if I was mutilated?
You cackled to winds.

You had authority. You had the scribes
falling at your feet waiting to
lap up words
gushing out your lips.

You made sure they recorded your views.
Not mine.
Never mine.
They weren't there. They didn't see.
Never knew me.
Only heard your words much later.

Did you stop to ask folks in the towns
we passed if they thought the same?
Could eyes be so deceiving everywhere?
But your words held sway.
Your truth had to do.
Their eyes were blinded with threats,
fear of fools that ruled.

It was the only way you could
start a war, coward that you were.
Get my brother to attack first, say it was his
fault, say he was vile, uncontrollable, lustful,
sinful, everything deceitful.

But I know,
your desire for me
destroyed my looks.
You couldn't bear to not have what
you wanted.
No control. Left your wife at home alone.
Staring at her sister every day,
your brother's wife.
You couldn't have her.
Such a sad example for a man.

When I laughed in your face, rejecting
the ineffective thing in front of me, the puny
man not even the deer in the woods
took notice of,
that was the last straw.
Out roared your fury.

Your sword. My nose.

I didn't deserve punishment, banishment
thrown out of my house, reviled by
the times to come.
I endured it all.
Through the ages my name rang
true peeling off the layers of lies,
and the future will learn.
Someday they will know.

I was beautiful.

On a Street in London

Watermelons jostle
inside the telephone booth too small to hold
such wonders overflowing their space.

Glass and steel surround him
with a view of the street beyond.
They stare at him defiantly at
eye level sticking out strong and proud.

Watermelons big,
watermelons small,
watermelons cheap,
come buy my wares, a business card
stuck to the side cries out to the world.

Lonely hearts stir at the sight
every time they glance inside.

Her eyes beckon, pick up the phone and
dial me in, they blink lustily, as
watermelons heave inside tomato red spandex
stretched to accommodate.

Tiny shivers run marathons down
his spine as he envisages the feel of it
in his palm yet dares
not lift a hand to touch.

Too many eyes watching silently as
footsteps tap around him.

The city drifts this way and that as he stands
still, inside the box in the middle
of the pavement watching her globes
straining to jump out.

Her voice purrs at the other end,
trembles down the line, he
listens mesmerized and
imagines the thousands of possibilities
squashed between watermelons
brown like the earth, trembling
like an earthquake.

Notes on the Poems

p.7 - On the Way Home
On December 16, 2012 a young woman returning
home after a late night movie in Delhi, India, was
gang raped on a bus and thrown onto the road.
While her name was withheld, she was referred to
as Nirbhaya – fearless.

p.43 – Sigiriya
Reference to the celestial maidens painted on the
walls of the rock fortress of Sigiriya, Sri Lanka,
during the reign of King Kashyapa 477 -495 CE.

p.65 – Fault Lines
The reference is to Sita who accompanies her
husband Rama and his brother Lakshman when
Rama goes into exile for 14 years, abandoning his
claim to the throne of Ayodhya, in ancient India.
Rama is considered as the seventh avatar of God
Vishnu. When Rama goes into the forest behind a
deer, Sita who is home becomes impatient and
wants him to return. Lakshman agrees to go look
for him, but because he doesn't want to leave Sita
alone he draws a line round the hut they live in
and tells her that as long as she stays within the
line she will be protected. This line is referred to as
the Lakshman Rekha. While the men are away
Ravana comes disguised as a mendicant and Sita
steps over the line to offer him food. Ravana is said
to have abducted her. Accompanied by an army of
monkeys Rama goes in search of her. When they
return to Ayodhya the citizens are supposed to have
questioned Sita's chastity and Rama orders her to
undergo a trial by fire to prove her chastity.

p.81 –Lines of Control
Reference to the Lakshman Rekha. According to the
Ramayana, Lakshman cut off the nose of
Suparnakha, sister of Ravana who tries to entice
Rama and Lakshman when they were in the forest,
or so it is claimed.
Reference to Draupadi, the most important female
character in the Mahabarata. She is married to the
five Pandava brothers. Yudhisthira pawns her after
he loses everything, including their kingdom, in a
game of dice. But Draupadi questions how he can
pawn her when he has lost himself first.
Reference to the statue of Aphrodite of Milos and
Helen of Troy.

p.93 – Goddess in Chains
Reference to Draupadi and it is about the moment
when she is pawned. Ordered by Duryodhan to be
disrobed, Dushasana unwraps her saree. But
Draupadi prays to Krishna to protect her and a
miracle occurs, resulting in her saree getting
extended so much that Dushasana stops exhausted.

p.117—A Princess Wronged
Reference to Suparnakha, sister of Ravana, Princess
of ancient Sri Lanka. According to the Ramayana,
Lakshman cut off Suparnakha's nose, and this lead
to a series of events that ended with the Indian
invasion and destruction of Sri Lanka.

About the Author

Shirani Rajapakse is a Sri Lankan poet and author. She won the *Cha "Betrayal" Poetry Contest 2013* and was a finalist in the *Anna Davidson Rosenberg Poetry Awards 2013*. Her collection of short stories *Breaking News* (Vijitha Yapa 2011) was shortlisted for the *Gratiaen Award.*

Rajapakse's work appears in many international publications including, *Flash:The International Short-Short Story Magazine, Litro, Silver Birch, International Times, City Journal, Writers for Calais Refugees, The Write-In, Asian Signature, Moving Worlds, Citiesplus, Deep Water Literary Journal, Mascara Literary Review, Kitaab, Lakeview Journal, Cyclamens & Swords, New Ceylon Writing, Channels, Linnet's Wings, Spark, Berfrois, Counterpunch, Earthen Lamp Journal, Asian Cha, Dove Tales, Buddhist Poetry Review, About Place Journal, Skylight 47, The Smoking Poet, New Verse News, The Occupy Poetry Project* and in the following anthologies, *Flash Fiction International (Norton 2015), Ballads (Dagda 2014), Short & Sweet (Perera Hussein 2014), Poems for Freedom (River Books 2013), Voices Israel Poetry Anthology 2012, Song of Sahel (Plum Tree 2012), Occupy Wall Street Poetry Anthology, World Healing World Peace (Inner City Press 2012 & 2014)* and *Every Child Is Entitled to Innocence (Plum Tree 2012).*

Rajapakse has a BA in English Literature (University of Kelaniya, Sri Lanka) and MA in International Relations (Jawaharlal Nehru University, India). She worked as a journalist, researcher and in international development before becoming a creative writer. An animal lover and vegetarian she loves to travel. Rajapakse lives in the suburbs of Sri Lanka's capital Colombo.

Afterword

Dear Reader,

If the poems in this collection touched you in any way, if they brought a smile to your lips or if they made you think and wish you could do something to change the way women are treated, let's start talking about it.

Recommend this book to your friends, reader's groups and discussion boards and make it easier for more people to find this book and join the discussion.

Review this book and let other readers know what you enjoyed about *Chant of a Million Women* and why. Leave the review on the retail site you purchased this book from or on Goodreads.

Visit my website for links to poems and stories published in literary journals and anthologies and sample other poems at Poem Hunter.

Connect on Facebook or follow me on Twitter, Pinterest, Instagram and LinkedIn to find out what's happening and to get notifications about new releases and giveaways. Or drop me an email.

Thanks for your support.
Sincerely,

Shirani Rajapakse

shiranirajapakse@gmail.com
shiraniraj@hotmail.com
https://shiranirajapakse.wordpress.com
https://www.facebook.com/shiranirajapakseauthor/
https://twitter.com/shiraniraj
https://www.pinterest.com/shiraniraj/
https://www.instagram.com/shiranirajapakse/
https://lk.linkedin.com/in/shiranirajapakse
https://www.amazon.com/Shirani-Rajapakse/e/B00IZQRAOA